I0412657

Life Between **Two Worlds**
1923-**2010**

Life Between Two Worlds
1923-2010

History is a reminder of human behavior

HORST UHSE

authorHOUSE®

AuthorHouse™
1663 Liberty Drive
Bloomington, IN 47403
www.authorhouse.com
Phone: 1-800-839-8640

© 2011 by Horst Uhse. All rights reserved.

No part of this book may be reproduced, stored in a retrieval system, or transmitted
by any means without the written permission of the author.

First published by AuthorHouse   11/07/2011

ISBN: 978-1-4670-4411-0 (sc)
ISBN: 978-1-4670-4410-3 (ebk)

Library of Congress Control Number: 2011917787

Printed in the United States of America

Any people depicted in stock imagery provided by Thinkstock are models,
and such images are being used for illustrative purposes only.
Certain stock imagery © Thinkstock.

This book is printed on acid-free paper.

Because of the dynamic nature of the Internet, any web addresses or links
contained in this book may have changed since publication and may no longer be
valid. The views expressed in this work are solely those of the author and do not
necessarily reflect the views of the publisher, and the publisher hereby disclaims
any responsibility for them.

CONTENTS

ACKNOWLEDGMENTS

There are many reasons to write of things that are of interest in life. The foremost of these reasons is my family, who for me sustain the meaning of life. Therefore, with the utmost love, I acknowledge my children—Gisela, Heidie, Peter, and Frank "the All American". My grandchildren—Patty, Mark, Gregory, Nicole, Cindy, George, Jr., Tony, Derek, Tracy, Melanie, Ryan, Matthew, Karlie, and Kerrie. And, my great-grandchildren—Chelsey, Alison, Kayla, Andrew, Jacob, Brooke, Dominic, Christina, Jack, and Ava. I wish to thank them all for the countless happy memories and joy they have given me.

I thank my children for their support and encouragement to write this manuscript. I wish to thank all of the wonderful people who have married into our family to add to our love and happiness.

There are also people outside of this family who are close to my heart. My thanks to the people of Grosse Ile, Michigan, who gave us their welcoming love and support when we immigrated to America.

Thank you to the people in Aliceville, Alabama, who gave us hope and understanding when we were prisoners of war.

Finally, thanks to all of my friends for their loyalty during the last fifty years. And special thanks to my good friend, Claus Wutherich, who helped me when I needed it the most.

Life is wonderful when you have a family that generates love and friends that last a lifetime. I will never take life for granted as I have learned that we all live under God's direction and destiny.

DEDICATION

*To my daughters, Gisela and Heidie,
my sons, Klaus-Peter and Frank,
and to all of my grandchildren and great-grandchildren.*

FOREWORD

My dear children, grandchildren, and great-grandchildren,

When I decided to write my autobiography in order to tell you something about my life, I did not realize that so many years have passed at lightning speed. Life itself is like a mountain surrounded by valleys. Sometimes you find yourself at the top of the mountain, other times you are mired down in the valley with no hope of ever reaching the top again. However, with strong determination, every man can defeat the obstacles in his path to accomplish the goals he has set for himself.

Today I look with immense pride at all of you, my children, and see how you have molded into beautiful people; each of you with the love and support of your spouses and each other have set your own standards to succeed in life and be role models to your own children.

I hope that you will love this little book and the man who has nothing to give you but his love.

THE MATERNAL WONDER

Although I did not know it at the time, January 6, 1923, was the most exciting day of my life. I succeeded in the maternal wonder—I was born. And so began my eighty six year-long journey to find out about all of the ups and downs this life on earth has to offer.

I grew like a weed and almost before I learned to crawl, I began to walk. My mother, Charlotte Brinke, was very young when she had me. I can still see her in my mind's eye; she was very pretty. Soon she was to leave me, giving me to foster parents.

The first of the families to foster me was named Bartold. I did not like it there. The Bartolds had four children of their own and life in their apartment could be quite hectic at times. I was considered an outsider by the other children and when they got into trouble; I was blamed, which led to me taking the beatings meant for them. The Bartold children wore the clothing that my mother sent for me, and I had to wear their old clothes and shoes with holes in them. One day, my mother paid a surprise visit to my foster home. When she saw what was going on she packed up my clothes and took me to Grandma's house.

The following day, my mother brought me to another foster home. Mr. and Mrs. Mond were wonderful people and I was very happy living with them for the next two and a half years. I was five years old by the time my mother, whom I barely knew, came to pick me up from the Mond's house to take me to the faraway place she called home.

My separation from the Mond family was very traumatic for me and I cried most of the 150 km train ride. A man sitting across from us tried to keep me quiet with a chocolate bar, but was not successful.

Finally we arrived at our destination—Teuplitz Niederlausitz Kr. Sorau. Herr Droge was the name of the man who picked up my mother and me in a carriage pulled by two horses. He was very nice to me and I felt drawn to him, calling him uncle. He taught me many things and we became very close.

Eventually, we stopped in front of a large house with a butcher shop in front. I asked my mother why we were stopping there. She replied that this was going to be my new home from now on and urged me to come inside to meet my new daddy. I told her that I thought my father was in America. My mother explained that I had a new daddy who was much better than the other daddy was. I was confused by this information, but soon felt much better when I came face to face with him. He said there is my little piepmatz, I gave him a big smile and ended up on his lap.

Many days went by until I met my first boyhood friend. His name was Werner Brendel. Werner was epileptic and had to be watched all of the time so he would not hurt himself. When I grew a little bigger, I was always at his side, like a mother hen, protecting him from injuries.

Werner's parents had a farm and I spent many happy days there. I especially loved the animals. All of the cows, pigs, and goats had names. I was amazed at the way they could communicate with people and how they would come to you when you called them. I had the most fun during hay season. Werner and I would sit atop a wagon pulled by two steers buried up to our necks in hay. Werner and I would remain close friends until I was drafted into the army.

Life was much slower in those days, and people much closer to the earth and to each other. On the first day of May, or Mayday, people would decorate their horses and wagons with little birch trees, putting benches all around the insides of the wagon, and drive on into the blue as they called it. Sometimes there would be a whole wagon train filled with music, food, and laughter.

1923 THE FINANCIAL COLLAPSE OF GERMANY

I was just born and had never experienced the aftermath of a financial disaster. Once I grew up and found out for myself, how a financial collapse can tail spin a country, leaving devastation in its wake.

The American dollar went from 7,225 mark to 4 trillion 210 billion 500 million mark. Later on, the Rentenmark was put into circulation. The mark was devaluated and the exchange rate was valued at 420 marks, it is very hard to describe the most devastating time this Country has ever seen.

A newspaper in the morning cost 50,000 marks, in the evening 100,000 marks. The cost of a pair of shoelaces would have bought an entire shoe store, in normal times. A loaf of bread and a bottle of milk rose to billions of marks. The wages could not keep pace with the rising prices. The women would go to the Factories two or three times a week to pick up their husbands' paychecks and then rush to the store and buy anything they could lay their hands on, whether they needed it or not. Many times, when they had to stand in line, the money lost its value and they had no milk for the baby and no bread for their husband's lunch. The people suffered in many walks of life, mostly the seniors, they lost their life saving and their pensions were worthless. Investments lost all of their value, the people were bewildered and hopeless and many took their own lives.

This was the ideal time for Hitler to put his foot into the political arena, as he knew the German people needed someone to lift them out of this dilemma. And, as history proved, that is exactly what happened. The republic, under Stresemann, went through a turbulent time. Trouble would linger in every part of the country. The separatists would stir things up in the Rhineland.

The communists[5] would clash with the opposition in Sachsen and Thüringen and Franken. Bayern and Württemberg were the cornerstones for Hitler's Nazis. From now on, politics and power play ushered us right into the 1929 depression. It was a very cold winter, 2.5 million people were unemployed. By 1930, unemployment grew to 5 million people. Able-bodied people that worked all their lives turned to Hitler out of frustration. He promised them a better future. Those without income pawned their possessions, families drew closer together and people in the country sent food to their relatives in the city.

In all that chaos, people were tired of the fighting and killing in the streets, the constant battles between the Nazis and the communist and all the demonstrations and police raids. The people yearned for some kind of authority and Hitler was their man, who would bring law and order back to the country. The German people had no idea that they made a decision they would regret for the rest of their lives.

Yes, history is a reminder of human behavior, and our behavior is not always to our advantage. Today we are facing a similar situation here in America and I hope that everybody has learned from this dilemma, you cannot spend more then you have. I know we are the biggest credit holder, but you know, the day will come when we have to give it all back. And, unless we accept that, greed will consume us and we will lose all of our profound principles. Why in God's name are we here on earth for? Think about it, we can still change it.

TRAVELING THE COUNTRY

Summer arrived and we knew we would soon be on summer vacation, a fun time for all the kids. We all had to join the Hitler youth, which is very similar to the American Boy Scouts. We would go on big camping trips cross-country. I remember I was 10 years old and this was my first trip, we were going to the Elb Sandstone Mountains and camp at the old castle of Koenig stein, one of the many castles of August, the strong one, the King of Saxony, it was great to see all his 365 uniforms, one for each day.

Everything was built with big boulders; a wall four feet thick surrounded the castle. When we looked over the wall, we could see all the little villages in the valley.

Inside the castle was a well that was so deep, if you throw a stone in you had to count to seven before you could hear the splash. The following day we broke camp and visited the castle of Lilienstein. Here, we went to the torture chamber deep down in the dungeon, it was terrible the way they tortured people in those days.

Well, we were ready to move on to our next vacation spot, but this time we had to make camp in the middle of the woods. We picked an open area so we could build a fire to cook our meals.

I was the youngest in our tent and elected to be the first guard. Guess what went through my mind? Snakes? Skunks? Or maybe even a wolf? Nah, just walk up and down and whistle and everything is going to be all right. After two hours, my relief was on its way and I went to get some shuteye.

Early in the morning, sixty boys ran to a nearby lake for a swim. When we returned, we packed our clothes and tents and hiked ten kilometers to the nearest town where we stayed for two days in a jugend Herberge. This is a building for young people and hikers to stay overnight and receive a free meal.

After two days we were rested enough to make it to the Isar mountains, sometimes in the afternoon we arrived in Bad Flinsberg. This was a town that I, later in my teen years, would pick as my winter vacation spot. When I returned home, my parents had tickets for the city theater in Cottbus, a sister theater of the Dresden Opera House. The operetta, The Bird Dealer, was a beautiful musical and the first one I had ever seen.

The Nieder Lausitz stretches along the Neisse River and is mostly farmland. People here work in general for all the big farms and their income is very meager, five marks a week is their normal income and town activity is about all they can afford. I didn't even realize how fortunate I was, our shoes were made by a cobbler, clothes made by a tailor and the clothes we didn't like anymore we would give to the poor and they would wear it on Sunday. However, I was about to find out what the real world looks like and only then was I able to survive the enormous challenges that this life put in my pass.

LIFE WITH MY STEPFATHER

My childhood with my Mom and new Dad was a happy one. I had a lot of friends, most of them I met in school. We had great teachers; they were very strict, but they helped every student to make sure they would pass their class. Some of the students had to stay over to get tutored for one hour, I was one of them! I had a lot of trouble solving math problems, I was happy that I passed on my report card with a C-.

We had homework every day. When I got home, I had to do my homework before I was allowed to go out and play. Mom would check my work to see if I did a bad job. If I didn't meet her expectations, I would have to do it all over again.

Life seemed very normal at our house until one day my happy life was clouded by fear. It turned out my Stepfather was a binge drinker and would not come home for three days. When he finally came home he would beat up on mom until she was green and blue in her face. She was not able to face the public for two weeks. My Stepfather always felt sorry afterwards and Mom forgave him, over and over again. From that day on, I started to dislike him.

My Mom sensed my behavior and told me that he adopted me and that he is my legal Father. Things were never the same after those episodes, I was growing up and my confirmation came closer for me to decide what I was going to do with my life. Some of my friends were planning to go to College I told my Mom that this is what I would like to do. My Stepfather, however, had different ideas. He wanted me to become a butcher. I hated the idea, but the case was closed, no debate allowed. After my three-years of training, at least I was allowed to go to a business school, even if only for the plans to take over the business later in my adult life.

But here came a big turnaround in my life, World War II broke out and my future was in limbo, only another year and I would have to face a war that nobody wanted.

THE WAR IN NORTH AFRICA

Hitler tried desperately to brainwash the German people to support his ideology and many people did for material gain or political beliefs. In many ways, Hitler did good in the beginning. He built homes for the poor people and built the Volkswagen for under a thousand Mark. It all sounded so good but turned into sour grapes and history explained all that.

The Polish war was in full swing and my Stepfather was called up for duty. I was left to run the Business at age 17 and, if I say so myself, I did a good job. Mom thought so too.

My Stepfather had a good friend who was an SS Sturmfuehrer. This man had enough pull to get my Stepfather back home, under one condition, that I take his place as a soldier in the Waffen SS, a branch of the SS troopers. But God was on my side, I was one centimeter too short to qualify and went into training under General Manteufel near Berlin, in a Kradschuetzen Regiment.

After our training, we were selected by General Rommel to enter the Africa Corp. We left from Potsdam by Berlin for Naples in Italy. Here we painted all our vehicles, tanks, motorcycles and guns in desert colors. Later all of our equipment was transported by ship to North Africa, we followed at a later date by air.

The time we had left in Italy turned out to be the last good days we would see for a long time to come. We were soon facing a war of uncertainty. Everybody was writing a letter home to their Moms and Dads to tell them not to worry.

In March 1942, we left Naples with 45 U52 transport planes, landing destination Tunis in Tunisia. Each plane was equipped with three machine-guns. It was our responsibility to defend the airplane, since we had only a pilot and a co-pilot.

Our flight was not without incident. British fighter planes attacked our formation, without success. The firepower of our planes was too overwhelming for three spitfires so they turned away never to be seen again. The pilot flew the aircraft as low as possible to prevent an attack from below.

We got closer to North Africa and had Cartage in site when the pilot received the order to change course and fly to a small airstrip near Gabes and wait for further orders. As we found out later, some of our planes had been shut up by French colonial troops at the Tunisian airfield. Even so, France had signed an armistice with Germany and was no longer at war.

The Prime Minister of France collaborated with Germany so the colonial troops would fight for Germany. Hitler promised the French Prime Minister that he would leave the North African territory untouched. The incident in Tunis was resolved and the Airport ended up in German hands.

Shortly after our arrival, General Eisenhower landed with a large force in Casablanca. Eisenhower was under heavy attack by French forces on land and sea. Three French patrol boats were sunk and many were taken prisoner.

After two days at the air strip, we were picked up by a unit of the 10th panzer division and transported to Ghudamis, a small border town on the Libyan Desert. We received our hardware on flatbed loaders; it sure felt good to be mobile again.

We received our first assignment, patrolling a ten-mile area to observe enemy movement. A British spearhead tried to attack our flank and create a bridgehead to cut off the supply line to our troops that were fighting in the Fuka position behind El Alemein. We moved out into the desert, supported by armored vehicles to attack a small armored column. We were quite nervous since this was the first engagement with a real adversary. I lit my first cigarette to calm my anxiety.

I heard the first roaring sound of our big guns and we knew then that we were in harm's way and had to defend ourselves if we wanted to stay alive. From that moment on, we all changed and our fight for self–preservation began. The fighting lasted for two days. The British lost numerous tanks and we lost nine good men that still weigh heavily on our minds. The British retreated, they knew we had strong forces in this area to prevent a bridgehead.

Gabes was under heavy attack by French forces who switched sides again. The Airport changed hands numerous times. We moved out and headed for Gabes and the French held a strong armored force around the airport that had to be crushed at all cost. We needed this airport to support our troops.

Fourteen tanks and a battery of 88 anti-tank guns was our convoy. British fighter planes had complete control over our air space and gave us a lot of trouble, they were like yellow jackets—you could not get rid of them. We could not afford to lose our equipment. We moved into Gabes early in the morning, we heard some machine-gun fire and knew that they were sitting ducks, waiting for armored support. We just got into position and when we received mortar fire we unleashed a quick response from our 88 guns and our mark IV 5cm guns. This silenced them very quickly. The French tanks were no match for our 88 guns and they capitulated. Moments later British lightnings bombarded the airport and destroyed two runways, air defense was put into place to keep the airport operational.

We spent four days cleaning up the mess and repairing the runways so our planes could land. I know many things happened in between I don't remember any more.

Rommel moved closer and closer to Tunisia. The British could not be stopped anymore. They had, by far, more equipment. Hundreds of tanks pushed us closer to Tunisia. We had no vehicles or tanks left and the Infantry was doomed. Thousands were taken prisoner. Our battle group was ordered to Ponte Fahs to confiscate as many civilian trucks as possible. Ponte Fahs had a huge petrol dump that we needed very desperately.

We confiscated 23 trucks and loaded them with barrels of gasoline. I would like to mention here that both sides benefitted from this petrol dump. The Arabs were the go between, to make sure we wouldn't confront each other.

All this gasoline would not help us anymore, the Panzer Divisions had hardly any tanks left to fight a war and trucks that would run were nowhere to be found. Things got ugly around Ponte Fahs and the British were pushing in every part of the African theater, we knew the war could not be won.

The rain made life even more miserable, we were cold and hungry. The Arabs gave us cornbread to eat but we didn't have enough saliva to swallow the bread.

We received a report from the Arabs that paratroopers had landed near Ponte Fahs. We responded immediately to the threat but the Americans were not well prepared for this operation and almost 50 paratroopers were taken prisoner and had to be released later.

The 10th panzer division arrived, including some of the new tiger tanks. Every remaining panzer division that had any tanks left, every motorized unit, everybody that had two legs was thrown into this battle at Tebourba to defend Tunis. Only a handful of guard troops were left behind.

The battle against the British 11th Brigade, the American Invasions force, the African Stalingrad raged for four days. the allies lost over 130 Tanks in the Tebourba area and many more in other areas.

Human losses were high on both sides, our battle group shrunk to 40 men. Even so, the battle was won, but the victory was short-lived. Eisenhower had a war machine that could not be stopped.

After the allies regrouped, they counterattacked and Tunis was lost. We pulled back to Hammamlif, but heavy artillery fire and low flying fighter planes made it almost impossible to protect ourselves or form a defense line. The British Navy kept us under fire day and night. We retreated to the halve Island of Cap Bone. My war buddy, Tony, and I were separated from our troops and approached a group of paratroopers. We gathered between two hills as a Colonel tried to regroup all the soldiers that were separated from their units, but it did not materialize. Heavy carpet-bombing and artillery fire made it impossible to create a defense line. Everybody was on their own. We stayed in a foxhole, but it was only a matter of time before the war would be over.

The war in this region ended in May 1943. We crawled out of our hole and saw the first American troops approaching. They seemed very happy that the war was over. They gave us some c-rations and told us to keep our weapons for self–protection. We were so surprised and expected something completely different.

We started moving in the direction of Tunis and couldn't believe our eyes when we saw the 100 artillery pieces that pounded our position for days. We walked for 60 miles. My knees were swollen and I was in pain, having injured them when I fell off an anti-aircraft gun during an air raid by British Spitfires.

However, God was always on my side—there it was—a big Austrian truck sitting on the side of the road. We investigated and found the truck was running and, to our amazement, loaded with beer salami and chocolate. I was sitting in the truck thinking about what my Mom once said to me when I was very rebellious. "There will be a day when you want to come home, but you can't". I knew this was the time.

I would not see my Mom for a long time to come. I opened up a can of beer salami and ate a chocolate bar. I knew this was not very healthy for my digestive system—and how right I was!

As we drove through Tunis, the Arabs were waving at us. We had a good relationship with them in those days. Soon we arrived in Mateur. The Americans had a huge transit camp there that housed about 20,000 prisoners. We dismantled our weapons and scattered them all over the ground. After that, we filled our pans with beer salami and walked to the camp.

The Americans didn't waste any time moving us to different locations, since they were interested in getting us to America as soon as possible. We were transported to Constantine for interrogation, I don't want to get into details here—those are military procedures and of no interest to anybody.

After three days, we were loaded into French railroad cars. They were small boxcars and this is when our nightmare began. There were forty-five prisoners in one car. You could barely stand up and the temperature rose to 100 degrees Fahrenheit. There was no air from the outside. We became very sick. It was a horrible ordeal because the heat was unbearable. We had American c-rations with polluted water that made things even worse.

Everybody had diarrhea; the situation was inhumane under Moroccan control. When we arrived in Marrakesh, American military took over and things went back to near normal. Nevertheless, we were so sick and jaundice and malaria had taken its toll.

The Americans decided to ship us to America as soon as the West Point arrives. Within seven days we were on our way to our destination of Boston, in the United States.

Our quarters were at the bottom of the ship. We had many wounded men on board. The seven U-boat alarms made us quite nervous, since we were at the bottom of the ship and everybody else was on deck with their life preservers on. The guard told us not to worry, that the West Point is a fast ship and doesn't need a Destroyer escort.

After nine days, we finally arrived in Boston and were loaded on a train, destination unknown. A long train ride awaited us—not in boxcars—but in coaches with sleeping quarters. We were traveling as if we were on a vacation. A big African American always served us breakfast and dinner with a smile. The food was outstanding and our fear of mistreatment subsided.

The next day we arrived in Aliceville, we had no idea what part of the Country we were in until later. The guards were lined up with their guns drawn. People looked upon us with curiosity, which was of no interest to us. We were tired and fatigued, a bed and medical help is all we needed.

The march to the camp seemed endless. When we finally got there, we were separated and admitted to the hospital where I stayed for almost ten months. I would like to mention here the outstanding job Captain Klippen did to nurse us back to health.

After recovery, we were transferred to camp—B. There were fifty men in one barrack, with one thousand men in each camp.

Life was very normal in our camp, no political disputes, the food was very good, and everybody was busy making a life for himself. We all helped in beautifying our camp. With the cooperation of Colonel Prince, we were able to put a band together, create a theater, form a soccer team, and play in chess tournaments. With so many activities, there was no time to create unwanted scenes. Of course, we stood up for our country, our brothers and sisters, and fathers and mothers. It was our homeland; whether Hitler was in it or not.

We had educational classes with college credits in Germany. My favorite subject was fundamental questions of right and wrong. Subjects like a chess game; you can dissect it like a frog. This has taught me to analyze the difference between right and wrong regarding my country. In the end we are all wrong.

Sometime in 1944, we were transported by train to a small POW camp in the middle of a military facility in Gordon Johnston, Florida. We were able to walk around more freely within the military compound. We worked in warehouses, motor pools, PX kitchens, tugboats and mess halls.

When the war ended in 1945, things started to change. We learned from the time many of our privileges were taken away from us. We were not going to let this happen again, so we emptied the canteen and buried everything from chocolate to cigarettes. Bacon and ham were nailed to the bottom of the tabletops in the mess hall. Of course, the guards with their steel pokers found many items outside, but they never found the bacon!

Life was not the same anymore, the war was over and we wanted to go home, but instead we were transported to Telogia, a camp that consisted of tents. We were cutting timber; the quota was three cords a day. If you cut less than that, you had to work on the weekend. I worked every weekend. Thank God we stayed there only for a short time before we were transferred to Fort Benning. We stayed there for three days and then we went on to camp Shanks in New York before leaving for England for another 18 months in captivity. Life was not easy then.

Aliceville will always be in my heart; it gave me another chance at life. Yes, America, you have been good to me and I thank you for it.

Maybe one day the world will love each other and live together in peace. I salute the people in Aliceville, Alabama, and all the people that contributed to the museum. Hopefully, our future generations will learn from this.

Our journey from New York to England was quite exciting. After almost an entire day of cruising, the old Liberty ship broke down and a repair ship, deployed from New York, had to sail out to repair the ailing vessel. The ship was sold to France for coastal duty after they dropped us off in Liverpool.

We avoided being taken prisoner by the British in North Africa, but now we had to face the music. We knew we were not very well liked by the British and expected that things were not going to be as it was in America, so we braced ourselves for a tough time in England.

Our thoughts proved to be right, the exact words from the Intelligence Officer, "we will give you tea and bread, but if you do not obey our rules, we can lay you in chains". That is, when I got naughty and spit on his shoe, I was then rewarded with a 28-day calaboose, an outstanding regimen for losing weight. After this little ordeal, I worked in a gypsum mine, underground. Not exactly in accordance with the Geneva Convention, but then again, what country ever did obey the rules. Our main menu was cabbage, day in and day out, but I could not eat that stuff, no matter how hungry I was. Therefore, I improvised and went into the house shoe business, which was flourishing and gave me other food items to survive.

The British women liked my pom–poms and I developed quite a little business. Later I added pillow tops and they were going like hot cakes! I used all the materials I brought home from the mine, like old transmission belts to make soles out of and transmission ropes that had white cotton inside which I stained into different colors and braided, and then started production.

Life in England was very boring, no activity of any sort. All except chess, which I pursued vigorously and gave me the opportunity to play a grand Master from the famous Hastings club in Sussex.

Our P.O.W. camp was located in an old historical Castle called Normanhurst, near the Town of Battle. It was quite interesting to have an inside look at how royalty lived at one time.

Time was passing us by and one day a rumor went around, that the British were going to send us home. The excitement was unbelievable and I wrote my mother to give her the good news. To my disappointment, I was not in that first group and had to wait another six months.

Finally, the day arrived and we were repatriated back to Germany on June 25, 1947. When we returned we were overwhelmed by the destruction. All of the cities were a pile of rubble. A great sadness overcame us and many had tears in their eyes.

LIFE IN GERMANY AFTER WORLD WAR II

When we arrived in Hanover, we received our discharge papers and our first food ration cards. Our train tickets were good until Nienburg, from there we had to hitchhike to Eystrup, the town my Mother told me to go to. Many Russian prisoners had to be carried to the main road because they were unable to walk. A British truck picked us up and dropped everybody off at their destination.

Eystrup was a long and narrow town. Friends of my parents who had a Textile company in our neighboring town, fled to Eystrup when the Russians came. These are the people that I was to meet, to help me get settled in Eystrup. Things like finding a bed or a room were very difficult.

I ended up in a Hotel where I spent all the money that I had saved in America. Was I directed here to meet the love of my life? It had to be! I met a young girl that seemed very withdrawn and quiet. She was pretty and of great interest to me. After many attempts, I finally had a chance. I saw her at a dance, was able to make a date with her, which developed into a relationship growing ever close.

I was financially not in the position to stay any longer at the Hotel, so the Burgermeister was responsible to provide a room and a bed with a straw sack and I moved into the Postmasters house.

On a Monday morning I was still in bed when someone knocked on my window. I jumped out of bed wondering who that could be. When I opened the curtains, I could not believe it, my Mom looked in back at me. I have never been so happy in all my life, I opened the window jumped out and took her in my arms, holding her for God knows for how long.

Now things started to get crowded in that little 9' x 9' room and I had to fight for a bigger room. I finally got after many trips to the Burger master. Mom told me the story of how she was guided by a young boy across the East German border in the middle of the night. It was a very dangerous undertaking but, thank God, she was safe now. Grandma went through a terrible time when the Russian troops occupied our town and she fled to Berlin. Soon the Russians arrived in there, and the Cossacks raped many German women. Grandma jumped out of a two-story building to get away from the Cossacks and fled to a nearby town.

Surprises were always knocking on our door, but this time it was the stork. Many thoughts went through my mind, for instance, how am I going to support a wife and child? I could barely support myself, but Else was so grown up, she said to me, "if you love me, we will go through life in thick and thin", and we did.

Finally, the day came for Else to have the baby. I was very nervous since, in those days, you had your babies at home with a midwife. Men did not get educated in that field like today, we learned the hard way. Everything went well and the baby was born. The Midwife said what a beautiful child, and I was very excited about my first child.

We needed a bigger place to live and through some organization, we got a three-room apartment in the next town, three kilometers away. Before we moved, we got married and Gisela got baptized. She sang the whole time we were in Church and even the Priest had to smile and said she must be really happy to be alive. We had two more children, one girl, Heidie, and a boy, Klaus-Peter. I loved my children. I always wanted at least three children because I didn't have any brothers or sisters and I always felt lonely all by myself.

Times in Germany were very depressing, the future seemed to be unreachable and you had the impression of a lost nation that had the disapproval of the whole World. The Holocaust created a guilt complex in all of us, we had no explanation, nor could we be held responsible for the terrible crimes that were committed. The majority of the people did not know the concentration camps existed. I had the opportunity to visit Dachau and a chance to talk to a man that lived there all of his life. He did not know that there was a concentration camp in Dachau because there was a no-man's land between the camp and the town. People knew something was going on there, but they didn't know what. I am going to leave this subject, since I had no intention of bringing politics into this book.

During my time in Germany I worked mostly for the British Army, a German Service Organization that worked for the British, as well as the American Military. My job was ninety kilometers from home and I came home only on weekends. Sometimes I rode my bike all the way home and even beat the train, because I had to wait six hours for the next train home.

In 1955, we applied for a visa to come to the United States; the World Church Service would pay for the trip and try to find a sponsor for us. The investigation took two years because I was a prisoner in two countries including Germany, as my home residency.

In 1955, I changed to a new job in Nienburg to be closer to home. I did the accounting for petrol and oil for the 21 Field Regiment. I worked there until we immigrated to the United States in September 1956. We sold our few belongings so we could pay for all the necessary expenses, including train fare.

After the Investigation by the INS, which Mom and I passed with flying colors, we were welcomed to the United States and had to report to the INS. In Bremerhaven, our ship, the General Langfitt, was waiting to take us across the ocean, to a new land that one day we would call our home. Mom and the kids had to stay in the lower quarters overnight while I went to the ship for orientation. I signed up to make my first American dollar, since I had only four dollars in my pocket—quite a gamble with a family of five.

Mom and I were solid like a rock that could weather any kind of storm, and, as it turned out later, we did. It was a deep hole, but we finally got to the top. It is so much easier to go from rags to riches than it is to go from riches to rags. I had to learn an awful lot to master life, rather than have everything handed to me. Mom came from a poor family and was a great teacher who taught me how to live a normal life without all the luxury and with less money.

LIFE IN AMERICA

Our cruise across the Atlantic was a disaster. We ran into a big storm of hurricane strength, and everybody was sea sick. Mom and the girls filled up paper bags all day and night. Little Peter couldn't understand why everybody was so sick, he said daddy and I feel fine. All the people that worked on the ship had permission to see the captain on the bridge and, oh boy, what a sight. The ship was more under water then above! I talked to one of the stewards that crossed the ocean many times, and he had never seen so many people sick then on this cruise.

I had never received so many hugs from strange people who got lost on the ship and could not find their cabin. After eleven days of battling the weather, we finally laid anchor in New York. After passing the Statue of Liberty, everybody was on deck to get a glimpse of the city with its high-rise buildings.

After several hours, we left the ship and boarded a train to Monroe, Michigan. When we arrived in Monroe, we were welcomed by two women from the Afternoon Guild of St. James Church. They told us that we were going to the chapel in Grosse Ile. First, to meet Reverend Hackwell, and then on to our final destination.

The people could not believe how well behaved our children were after that long train ride, but it didn't take them long to get Americanized. They learned very fast, if you are in America do as the Americans do.

Mrs. Owen, the staff woman, told us that a house had been rented for us on 7th Street, off of Bellevue. The house had been painted, decorated, and furnished. As we went inside, it looked like a dollhouse and we all had tears in our eyes when we saw that the kitchen cabinets were full of food along with every little item that you would need in a modern household. It was like a fairy tale and we would never forget that moment. The Grosse Ile community will always be close to our hearts.

Life in a new Country had begun, and now it was time to get a job. The job market was not very good at this time, but I landed a job at a Volkswagen dealer in Detroit as a parts manager. This didn't last very long and I did not earn enough money to support a family of five.

Mr. Owen, who was our first American friend, got me a new job at McLouth Steel Corporation. It was not exactly what I was looking for, but it paid enough money to support my family.

While I was working in Detroit, I had the opportunity to buy a car for a hundred dollars. The car was a 1949 Dodge coup and it looked like it came right off the assembly line; although it used to belong to an elderly man who bought the car and never had a chance to drive it because he lost his eyesight. When I brought the car home for the first time, Mom thought I had lost all of my senses and said, "Where in God's name did you get the money from to buy this new car?", and you guessed it, I had some explaining to do. I paid the car off in ten installments. Since the car was only a two seater, I had to arrange to get the whole family inside. We had two children's chairs that we put behind our seats that served as the seating arrangement for the girls. Little Peter would sit on mom's lap—in those days that was not against the law because traffic was only a fraction what it is today.

In that first year, I met a lot of wonderful people in church. A German lady that lived in America all her life offered me two thousand dollars to buy a house if I promised to pay her back in five years. We bought an old house that needed a lot of work. Else and I knew we could make something out of this old house if we put our mind to it.

We completely gutted the house inside and then rebuilt all the walls and started to remodel. I wanted my children to be proud of their home. I did everything myself—wiring, plumbing, heating, and painting. I started in the spring with snow still on the ground, but, by October 10th, we turned the heat on. The inspection turned out flawless, the downstairs was completely done except for the painting.

The next job was the upstairs. This was a much bigger problem. The big radiators had to be carried down, and a big chute had to be built from the upper window into a trailer, to get rid of all the plaster and wood lath. Mom had white hair for two weeks from dumping plaster down the chute. I would have never been able to do it without her.

I worked way into the night to get it finished by Christmas. Mom would wake me up in the morning, make me breakfast, and see me off to work. It was a busy time, people would come by sometimes and ask me if I ever rested. We had no time to rest; we had things to do. We had to climb that ladder, to find out how far up it will go to reach the top.

We finally got to the finish line. The house was completely done inside; the only thing that was left was the appearance of the house outside, including the landscaping. I dug a sixty-eight foot foundation and built a new porch. For some of it, I had to pay a contractor. The house was dressed up with aluminum siding, the yard was all landscaped, the garage was rebuilt, and a driveway put in. We lived in this old house for 30 years. When I finally sold it, my grandchildren were very disappointed. They thought that all the good memories they had growing up there would be gone with the old house. When Christmas came they said that Christmas has never been the same since you sold that old house.

But nothing ever stays the same. Time was passing us by at lightning speed. The girls turned into two beautiful young women and the boys started knocking on our door. It was a frightening time for a Father, thinking about losing his little girls. My oldest son was a handsome looking young man and he was looking for a young woman for himself.

Before I knew it, they were all married and I became a grandfather. It was so very wonderful. They all turned out to be great kids, and I have every reason to be proud of them. And, even prouder still, when my grandchildren married and raised their children with our family traditions. I have never experienced a generation gap with any of my children because we were always there for them.

In 1989, after we sold our house, we built a ranch-style condominium on Grosse Ile. After four years, all of our friends moved to Florida and tried to convince us that we could live a lot cheaper there too. Since I retired in 1985 and was on a fixed income, I thought this was a good idea. We talked to our children and decided to sell the condo.

In 1993, I flew to Florida and bought a house exactly how Mom described she wanted the layout. Mom packed all the delicate items, I wrapped all the furniture with foam rubber, and off we went.

When we got to Florida and Mom saw the house, she was overwhelmed. She got lost in the house all the time and I always said, "wrong way, guy." Since Mom was an excellent swimmer, she loved the pool and never missed a day taking her hour-long swim. Later, we added solar heat so we could use the pool part time in the winter.

We lived there for nine years, but the house was too big to clean and we decided to scale down and build a smaller home. We looked at a model across the street and liked it very much. We made a contract with the developer and moved in at the end of 2001.

Wellington is a gated community and seemed to be a safe place to live. But I still missed my big house; it was so comfortable, I could do anything I wanted to do and didn't have to ask anyone. Here I am not allowed to do anything without permission, and I missed that short dip in the pool before bedtime. We do have wonderful neighbors though, and they really make up for everything.

The first year in Florida was a tremendous change on many levels, especially getting used to the climate and the severe storms. The first time we were hit by lightning, we lost our VCR, our television cable, and our rain sensor burned up. The second time was more serious; our oak tree got hit and burned a trail all the way under our Lanai, killing all of our plants inside. Our telephones burned up, the lightning arrester on the garage door opener, and the TV cable in the ground outside. All the connections inside and outside of the cable TV had to be changed. Now we have surge protectors on everything. I sure hope Mother Nature gives us a break this year.

Mom turned eighty-one on May 1, 2003. She is still very active, and teaches aerobics when the regular instructor is not available. The ladies here think she is just amazing because of the things she can still do at her age and how strong she is. The ladies like her because she knows the exercises by heart. While Mom is doing her aerobics, I spend 45 minutes in the exercise room. Then Mom and I swim for an hour. This keeps us fairly fit, which is important at our age.

Wellington is a very active, health-oriented community. It is amazing to see all the games played and the many exercise dances that are performed every day. The day starts early in the morning with a two mile walk, at 10:00 a.m. is bocce ball, at 11:00 am is tee off time for the men who prefer golf, or other sports such as tennis, horseshoes, or billiards. Then there are the red heats, the wanderers, the cruisers and the bingo fanatics. As you can see people are not dying of boredom; just cancer or old age. So what advice can I give the younger generation? Exercise and play into old age and never let the romance die. It will keep your heart young and healthy and your outlook on life positive.

The year 2003 started out wonderfully, but ended so tragically. Gisela's husband, John, died on June 5, 2003. It was a shock to all of us; he was still so young. John was a great father to his children and a loving husband. John's grandchildren adored him. He was always there for them. This would be a very sad Christmas for the Konwinski family. It still saddens me to think about it. Mom and I decided not to fly up to Michigan for the Christmas Holidays that year and spent Christmas in Florida instead.

The month of December, 2004, we booked a flight to Michigan to spend Christmas with our family. It was very exciting for us. It was going to be different this time, we would see all of our grandchildren and great-grandchildren and our thoughts were filled with joy.

When we arrived at Gisela's condominium, Mom had a hard time climbing the stairs and needed my assistance. I knew something was very wrong. I noticed already that something was not right in Florida, and wanted her to see a doctor. Her reply was, "I will when I get back." Mom always had her own mind and there was no way to convince her otherwise.

Christmas day was here and everybody was getting ready to go to Heidie's house for Christmas brunch. Mom was sitting in the living room, ready to go. Then I heard this frightening call. I ran into the living room to see Mom fighting for her life. I knew she was having a severe stroke. I held her hand and she was squeezing my hand back with all the strength she had left. Gisela called 911 and we rushed her to Oakwood Hospital. The rest of the family was notified and arrived less than 30 minutes later. It is very hard to write about this, but I wanted all the little ones to know what happened to their Grandma.

The Hospital staff led us into the conference room and we had a fast decision to make. To save Moms life, we had three choices: do nothing and just give her aspirin, do the normal procedure, or try something new—something that had been done only two times before—one success and one failure. We had no choice; we had to try the new procedure, which proved to be successful.

We had a long road ahead of us, but I was determined to rehabilitate Mom at all costs. We fought a 4-year long battle and her pain and suffering were beyond human endurance, it could not be described with words. This is a sad part for me and I am going to stop right here.

Several months passed before I was able to take Mom back to Florida. It was a long battle that we could not win. Mom closed her eyes forever on Christmas Eve 2008.

In December, 2009, my youngest daughter lost her husband, George, who was also too young to leave us so early. I went to Michigan to say my last goodbye. Wondering, why him? Is it because he has fulfilled his purpose on this earth? Is this why I am still here? Do I have more to do to complete my deeds? Many thoughts go through your mind when a loved one is taken from you too soon. You lose this person in so many ways, and every family member is affected by this loss. Heidie is a very strong person and doesn't show her emotion in public. She is just like her Grandfather in that way.

She has a strong determination to move forward and stay focused; only then can she be a role model to her children.

The year 2010 forced many of us to make changes. George's departure into God's Kingdom taught us that we are not the ones that make the decisions; but we are the recipients of God's love and direction. We all miss George a great deal, but if we go back just a few months, we can remember the wonderful times we had with him. The time at the cabin with all his grandchildren or on the boat with his buddy, Pete, and all of his friends are happy memories that will always stay in our hearts forever.

And now, my grandchildren and great grandchildren I will introduce you to a lady that you have never met before, my mother, Charlotte Brinke Uhse Grace. She was born March 8, 1903, in Breslau, Germany. Your aunt Gisela spent many happy days with her and can tell you a lot about her. She was a very energetic lady. At age 66, she still rode her bike from Taylor to Grosse Ile. I remember when I got married and your great grandma provided a pillow for us to sleep on. When your aunt Gisela was born, she cut up all her linen for diapers. She would go with us into the woods to collect firewood for the winter and sometimes take all you kids for a day if Mom and I wanted to go to a dance.

When we came to America, we had a two-year waiting period before we were able to sponsor your Great Grandma and bring her to America. She was married again here in America to Vincent Grace. They moved from Detroit to Taylor, Michigan. Vincent died on November 7. 1969. Grandma was still working in Birmingham as a private nurse until March 1, 1971. On her day off, March 3, 1971, she was murdered.

She was a beautiful lady and the picture on the next page will not do her justice.

History is a reminder of human behavior. Yes, we all have a history and our behavior is the slide rule for what we accomplish in life and how we defeat the obstacles that block our path.

Many times I have observed the way people react to their own demise; their life is so visible to the world. No, it shouldn't be that way. Our life should be invisible to the outside world and to show the strength within ourselves is to overcome adverse conditions and fight for a better tomorrow. The Lord says, "Don't worry about tomorrow, tomorrow will take care of itself." Well, hasn't it?

Life for me was like a roller coaster that reached all the way around the world and I had no way to stop it. Nevertheless, I know it will stop when I reach the destination that is designated for me. Moreover, when it does, a new life cycle will begin. Will it be any better? Yes, it's gotten better, but also with the same adversities. Life is never perfect, but neither are we.

Being happy with what God has provided for us is what real life is all about. When I grew up in a small town in the eastern part of Germany, life seemed to be like a paradise. But that all changed when I grew up. Time was not standing still. The age of Modernization began. Outhouses disappeared and were replaced by water closets. Farm equipment was modernized and horses were replaced by tractors. Time passed at a much slower pace. After the World War II era, the world evolved in a much faster speed that has not slowed down to this very day. In the last sixty years since World War II, our technology has reached a point that is almost beyond our imagination.

This enormous leap made me think about a time in England when a speaker from the Government said the following,"today we are controlling technology, but the day will come when technology is going to control us." We have reached that point today. Space exploration has given us a volume of information that has catapulted technology at a speed that is very frightening to us.

I don't live in Germany anymore. America is my new home, the land of freedom and wide open spaces. The years ahead of us will have good times and sad times. Building a new life in a new country is very challenging. To create a relationship with the American people was the most refreshing experience and I will never forget it. So little was known to the American people about our life under the rule of Adolf Hitler and there were many questions and answers.

Today I don't feel like an immigrant anymore. I am an American citizen and have many American friends, but the time of the holocaust still weighs heavy on our minds. Censored press prevented many German people from gaining knowledge of the terrible crimes that were committed.

Germany is, by name only, my birth country, since I have lived fifty-eight years in the United States. The rest of the time, I was in the military, outside of the country. Hitler forced many people into poverty when the war was lost and a big part of Germany was given to Poland.

Not a happy homecoming for me when I was repatriated from England with no home to go to, since my home was east of the Neisse River and now in Polish territory.

Even in America, life has sometimes bumpy roads, but overall I have a happy life here with all of my children.

Today we live under adverse conditions here in America. A deep recession has changed the lives of many people. Even in my own family unemployment has left its mark. The roller coaster is still going and will not stop until we reach our destination. Now we have reached a new cycle, life will be better again, but adversity will always be with us.

In my Retirement years, I traveled with my lovely wife to Europe and visited the Bavarian Alps, beautiful Austria, and Switzerland. Every country has its own beauty and if peace could be a global law, the World would be a paradise.

I live in Florida now. The warm climate seems to be better for my old bones. Life has lost all of its charm since my wife passed away in 2008 and this is the reason I wrote this little book.

This year was very exciting for me. I spent two months with my children in Michigan. We had three graduations in our family, my grandson, Ryan, and two of my great granddaughters, Chelsey and Alison. All three will go to college; they are great kids and have a great future ahead of them.

The tragedies in 2003 and 2009 have been devastating to my daughters; both lost their husbands at a young age and a father and grandfather to their children and grandchildren.

Our lives will always be full of adversity, but it is hope that keeps us going.

Life in Michigan was at a much faster pace than what I was used to. The kids were always on the go. We went to the cabin in Tawas, a beautiful little town in northern Michigan. The cabin is in the middle of the National Forest, nestled around a trout pond with a gazebo on it. It has beautiful scenery, the fire pit is always lit, and the music blasting into the night to keep the coyotes away. You feel so energized when all these trees surround you. Nature is such a wonderful creation that we should cherish and protect.

America is such a beautiful country and only a small percentage of people have ever seen the beauty of this great land, including myself. I have seen some parts of America, but have never seen the western states or parts of New England. Time or money was always an obstacle.

After several days in the wilderness, we returned to civilization. My grandson, Mark, who is a very talented drummer, already had plans for me; a concert in Milford, that we, of course, attended. Milford is a nice town and has one of the biggest street fairs that I have ever seen. The concert was performed in a huge tent that was visited by about 2,000 people. The band is so popular that Milford renews their contract every year.

The time of my stay has just about come to an end. My two sons, who are great cooks, prepared my fair well dinner for a party that everyone planned. It was a great time, but saying good-bye isn't always easy, thinking about going back to a lonely house. Everyone will have to face that someday. You can't prepare for something like that. It just puts you before the alternative; it is the hardest life cycle you will ever endure.

EPILOGUE

Life in Reverse

Life is a mechanism that stirs us from the day we are born until the day we leave this earth forever. There is not been enough time between youth and adulthood to think about what the future holds for us.

The years 2003, 2008, and 2009 were those years that made me realize that you cannot take life for granted without thanking God for every wonderful day that you have enjoyed with all of your loved ones.

When God opened the gate to heaven for John, Mom, and George, it was devastating to all of us. I knew we would never again hold them in our arms and tell them that we love them.

November 26, 2008, Mom and I had our 60th wedding Anniversary at the hospital and renewed our vows. Mom looked so happy that I kept my promise and she was looking forward to going home. God had a better home for her, a home with no pain, no suffering and with unconditional love. A home with everlasting peace; waiting for the moment to meet with me again.

Life is very lonely right now and has lost all of its glamour and luster. My energy and spunk for life has vanished. Material things do not mean much to me anymore and I don't know yet how I will cope in the future.

I have seen life in its utmost ugliest form and I knew what to do to survive, but now I don't know; it is harder than anything that I ever experienced, but with God's help I shall overcome.

My dear children, grandchildren and great grandchildren; this is the end. I hope it has given you a glimpse inside the man that began a new life in America with a family that I am very proud of.

The Author defines his story, whether it is written by thought or emotion. Biography is written by emotion, it portrays a story of his life that needs to be told, it fits our time. It is a story of a German immigrant that has lived under dictatorship and has endured a struggle from the day he was born, through World War II and later behind barbed wire as a prisoner of war here in America and in England.

He writes about his life after the War in Germany without any fascination. Life in Germany had lost its glamour. There seemed to be no future for his children that he loved so dearly. The time had come for him to go back to America, the land that he had learned to love. He knew that one day he would call this strange land home. The love and devotion of the American people was so energizing that he knew he was on the right path and his plans exceeded his expectations.

Life Between two Worlds is a story written with great emotion. It is told by a German Immigrant who has seen the obstacles that life can put in your path. Life in Germany under a dictatorship cannot be put in any kind of comparison.

As a small child, I already learned what hardship is by living with foster parents for two and one half years. My teen years were non-existent. World War II broke out and life was all rules and restrictions. Obedience was the first commandment.

As a soldier in the Africa Corp under General Rommel, I experienced the horror of War, a War we knew from day one could never be won. When the War ended in 1943 life behind barbed wire in the United States was the result of an irresponsible war.

When I returned to Germany in 1947, life was very depressing. Every city was a pile of rubble. My thoughts went back to America; to a land that I learned to love with its people who showed so much compassion for us when we were prisoners there. From that day on, I knew that I was going back to America to give my children a future. When I arrived with my family of five in New York with four dollars in my pocket, I knew that was all I needed to succeed.

www.ingramcontent.com/pod-product-compliance
Lightning Source LLC
Chambersburg PA
CBHW021247280526
45784CB00005B/2263

* 9 7 8 1 4 6 7 0 4 4 1 1 0 *